KU-021-723

KU-021-723

habitat explorer

# Desert Explorer

## Greg Pyers

Raintree

# www.raintreepublishers.co.uk

Visit our website to find out more information about **Raintree** books.

To order:

 Phone 44 (0) 1865 888112

 Send a fax to 44 (0) 1865 314091

 Visit the Raintree Bookshop at **www.raintreepublishers.co.uk** to browse our catalogue and order online.

Published in 2004 by Heinemann Library
a division of Harcourt Education Australia,
18–22 Salmon Street, Port Melbourne Victoria 3207 Australia
(a division of Reed International Books Australia Pty Ltd,
ABN 70 001 002 357).
Visit the Heinemann Library website @
www.heinemannlibrary.com.au

First published in Great Britain by Raintree,
Halley Court, Jordan Hill, Oxford OX2 8EJ,
part of Harcourt Education.
Raintree is a registered trademark of Harcourt Education Ltd.

A Reed Elsevier company

© Reed International Books Australia Pty Ltd 2004

08 07 06 05 04
10 9 8 7 6 5 4 3 2 1

All rights reserved. No part of this publication may be reproduced, stored in a retrieval system or transmitted in any form or by any means (electronic, mechanical, photocopying, recording or otherwise) without the prior written permission of the publisher.

Editorial: Carmel Heron, Sandra Balonyi
Design: Stella Vassiliou, Marta White
Photo research: Jes Sendbergs, Wendy Duncan
Production: Tracey Jarrett
Map: Guy Holt

Typeset in Officina Sans 19/23 pt
Pre-press by Digital Imaging Group (DIG)
Printed in China by WKT Company Limited

**National Library of Australia Cataloguing-in-Publication data:**
Pyers, Greg.
    Desert explorer.

    Bibliography.
    Includes index.
    For primary school students.
    ISBN 1 74070 141 0.

    1. Desert ecology – Juvenile literature. I. Title.
    (Series : Pyers, Greg. Habitat explorer).

577.54

## Acknowledgements

The publisher would like to thank the following for permission to reproduce photographs: Bruce Coleman Inc.: p. 18, /J-C Carton: pp. 19, 22, /Kenneth W. Fink: p. 10, /John Giustina: p. 29, /Giorgio Gualco: pp. 7, 26, /F. Jack Jackson: p. 25, /Joe McDonald: p. 23, /Michael Morecombe: p. 9; Corbis/© O. Alamany & E. Vicens: p. 17, /© Tiziana and Gianni Baldizzone: p. 16, /© Peter Johnson: p. 11, /© Wolfgang Kaehler: p. 14, © Royalty-Free: p. 8; Ecopix: p. 20; Victor Englebert: pp. 24, 28; Lonely Planet Images/Anthony Ham: p. 27; Natural Visions: p. 15; OSF Limited/© Alain Dragesco-Joffe: pp. 13, 21; photolibrary.com/Karl Ammann: p. 12; World Images/Ruth Lathlean: p. 5.

Cover photograph of camel reproduced with permission of Corbis/ © Jose Fuste Raga.

Every attempt has been made to trace and acknowledge copyright. Where an attempt has been unsuccessful, the publisher would be pleased to hear from the copyright owner so any omission or error can be rectified.

# Contents

Any words appearing in the main text in bold, **like this**, are explained in the Glossary.

# The Sahara Desert

Imagine flying in a helicopter over the Sahara Desert in North Africa. It is morning and there's not a cloud to be seen. Below are sand dunes as far as the eye can see. The helicopter slows and begins a descent. Here, the dunes have given way to a rocky plain. You are near the very heart of the largest desert in the world.

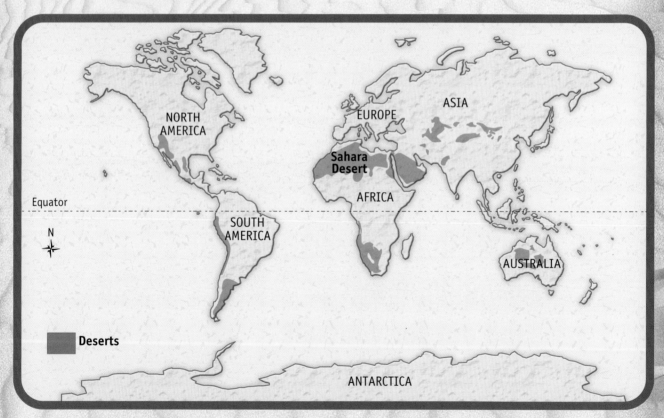

**This map shows the locations of the world's deserts. Deserts are very dry places found mainly in hot parts of the world.**

Sahara words:
- cloudless
- sandy
- warm
- clear
- **barren**
- dry.

# Desert habitats

The Sahara Desert stretches
5000 kilometres (3100 miles)
east to west and 1500 kilometres
(930 miles) north to south. Within this vast area,
there are many different kinds of desert **habitats**.
Habitats are places where animals and plants live.
These habitats are what you are about to explore.

A guide leading a camel team is waiting to take you.
He is eager to get started because although the
current temperature is a pleasant 25° Celsius, later in
the day it will soar into the high 40s. You mount your
camel and begin the journey.

# The heat of the day

You set out from the edge of a wide plain. It is covered in gravel, rocks and sand. To the west, the dunes look like large hills. To the east, rocky mountains stretch away to the horizon. Your guide leads off towards them.

The temperature is rising fast. The air is very dry. Apart from the camels, there are no other animals in sight. There aren't even any plants to be seen. The desert seems a lifeless place.

## Rainfall

Rainfall is less than 25 millimetres a year over most of the Sahara. In many places it may not rain for decades. In the mountains, enough rainwater collects for athel pines and acacia bushes to grow.

## Noon

At midday, you enter a narrow rocky gully. Your guide stops the camel team. It is 42° Celsius in the shade of a cliff. While you rest, the camels drink their fill from a rock pool. Rain must have fallen in the past day or two. If rain doesn't fall again soon, the rock pool will dry out in a few days.

The Hoggar Mountains in Algeria are a rocky part of the Sahara.

Explorer's notes

Desert landscapes:
- sand dunes
- mountains
- stony plains
- rocky gullies.

# The desert at night

Shadows lengthen as the sun sinks behind the mountains. The temperature falls. It is a good time to travel. It's also a good time for desert animals to come out to feed.

## Life after dark

In the dark, night-vision goggles help you to see. You put them on and immediately something catches your eye …

## Adaptations

Animals and plants have features that help them survive in the desert. These features are called **adaptations**. The big ears of a jerboa are an adaptation because as blood passes through them, heat is lost to the air and the animal cools.

It is a rat-sized animal, with hind legs like a kangaroo's. It's a jerboa, nibbling at a tuft of grass. It pauses frequently to sit up, to watch and listen for **predators**. Predators will be looking for **prey** such as jerboas to eat. The jerboa's large eyes help it to catch the weak light, its large ears the faintest sound. Suddenly, the jerboa bounds away and disappears down a burrow. Soon, you see why.

Explorer's notes

Jerboa adaptations:
- large eyes for night vision
- long legs for escaping from predators
- big ears for keeping cool.

A jerboa obtains all of its water needs from its food.

# Night-time predators

A fennec fox has appeared, too late to catch the jerboa. Its ears twitch as they catch a faint sound. The fox turns quickly and pounces. When it lifts its head, it has a gecko lizard wriggling in its jaws.

The fennec fox is the world's smallest fox.

## Nocturnal animals

Animals that are active at night are called **nocturnal** animals. In a desert, where water is so scarce, being nocturnal is an important **adaptation**. Very little water **evaporates** from an animal's body in the cool night air. During the day, the animals avoid the heat by sheltering in burrows or in dens among the rocks.

Midnight approaches and the air is very cool. Along the base of a crumbling cliff, a large, hairy animal is sniffing the rocky ground. It is a striped hyena, hunting alone for lizards and small **mammals**.

Hunting the same **prey** is a caracal, a cat with a short tail and tufted ears. The caracal stays far away from the hyena and disappears into the darkness.

This caracal leaves its den at night to hunt.

Explorer's notes

Desert night animals:
- jerboas
- fennec foxes
- gecko lizards
- gerbils
- spiny mice
- caracals
- striped hyenas.

11

# Early morning

By dawn, all of the animals seen the night before have returned to their burrows and dens. But it is still cool enough for many other animals to be active. In the shadows, there is a thin frost on the rocks. This formed when moisture froze in the cold night air.

A small herd of dama gazelles has appeared, searching for grass and straggly shrubs. One looks up. Now the whole herd is alert. They begin to run. A cheetah is sprinting towards them!

## Bobcats

In the deserts of south-western USA, bobcats prey at night and on cool days on small animals such as jackrabbits and kangaroo rats.

**Fleeing dama gazelles leap into the air to escape a cheetah.**

## Fast hunters

Cheetahs use speed to catch **prey**. At night it would be too dark for high-speed chases, so they hunt in the cool hours of the morning and early evening. With a swipe of a front paw, the cheetah trips a gazelle. The gazelle falls, breaking its neck. The cheetah pants to get its breath and keeps an eye out for any striped hyenas that may try to steal its catch.

Cheetahs of the Sahara prey mainly on gazelles.

### Explorer's notes

Cheetah prey:
- dorcas gazelles
- dama gazelles
- addax
- scimitar-horned oryx.

# Into the mountains

You are now 1000 metres above the plain. A group of small, furry animals on a rocky ledge is basking in the morning sun. These are rock hyraxes. High above, a tawny eagle is soaring on the warm air that rises from the rocks. The hyraxes haven't seen the eagle, but with their thickly padded feet, they can scurry back among the rocks very quickly. The eagle moves on, searching for easier **prey**.

The rock hyrax feeds on plants that grow in the cracks between rocks, where water collects.

## Journey across the Sahara

More than 180 **species** of birds migrate across the Sahara to and from Europe every year. These birds are not **adapted** to the desert climate. They can die of overheating or **dehydration**. The mountains provide shade, food and water.

# Visitors

A flock of small birds suddenly whirrs into the air. They rise quickly and then head south in a direct line. Their next stop may be hundreds of kilometres away, beyond the desert. These birds may have been larks, **migrating** from Europe to southern Africa. They had stopped to rest and feed in the desert mountains before completing their journey.

This swallow is crossing the Sahara on its migration from southern Africa to Europe.

### Explorer's notes

Migratory birds of the Sahara:
- wheatears
- warblers
- larks
- swifts.

# Desert plants

Out on the stony plains, there were no plants to be seen. Water is needed for plants to grow and the rainfall there is too low. Here in the mountains, rainfall is still very scarce – about 100 millimetres a year – but just enough for many plants to survive. There are even patches of grassland and woodland here. This is why more animals can live in the mountains than on the desert plains and dunes.

## Explorer's notes

Plants of desert mountains:
- acacias
- lavender
- figs
- grasses
- athel pines
- umbrella thorns.

**Acacia trees grow in the desert mountains.**

# Plant adaptations

Umbrella thorns are stunted shrubs, but they are well **adapted** to desert conditions. Their leaves are very small, so they lose very little water. They also have thorns to protect their leaves from hungry animals, such as gazelles.

The thorns of this umbrella thorn prevent animals from feeding on its leaves.

Each plant has a very long **taproot**, which reaches for moisture deep in the soil. Some umbrella thorns have taproots that are 30 metres long.

## Saguaro cacti

The 15-metre-tall saguaro cacti of the Sonora Desert, in the USA, store water in their fleshy stems. Sharp spines protect the stems from hungry animals.

# Clues to the past

You have arrived at a special place. Beneath a rocky overhang, there are paintings and engravings. The paintings were made with ochre, a coloured clay. The paintings and engravings show giraffes, rhinoceroses, hippopotamuses and other animals that don't live in the desert. But they did more than 5000 years ago, when the paintings and engravings were made.

**This engraving of a rhinoceros was made thousands of years ago.**

## Explorer's notes

Animals that have disappeared from the Sahara:
- rhinoceroses
- giraffes
- lions
- hippopotamuses
- ostriches.

These artworks show that long ago the Sahara was a **fertile** place with plenty of water. Since then, the climate changes turned it into a desert.

These rock paintings are in Algeria.

## Ancient survivors

In a narrow gully, a group of cypress trees over 2000 years old still survives. When they were seedlings, the climate must have been much wetter. Today it is too dry for the seeds of these trees to grow.

### Way back

Millions of years ago, rainforests and wetlands covered the land. A huge 20-metre-long dinosaur called jobaria roamed the land 135 million years ago. A dinosaur-eating crocodile called sarcosuchus lived here 110 million years ago.

# Life in the sand

A day later you are back at the edge of the dunes. There seems to be no life at all out here. But among the sand grains there are seeds. When it rains the seeds grow into plants that may cover large areas of the dunes. But the sand is constantly shifting and plants can't gain a permanent roothold here. So these plants are short-lived. They are also very small, to avoid being blasted by sand whipped up by the fierce winds.

**Grasses, such as wild oats, can grow where the dunes are stable.**

Addax are well adapted to hot, dry desert conditions.

# Addax

The only animals you see are a small herd of addax. These antelopes are the largest animals of the Sahara. They have broad hooves to keep them from sinking into the loose sand. They are also light-coloured, to reflect the sun's heat.

Addax rarely drink. They suck moisture from desert grasses and bushes. Addax sometimes dig **depressions** in the sand to shelter from the sun and wind.

## Explorer's notes

Addax **adaptations**:
- broad hooves
- light colour
- dig shelters
- need little water.

# Predators and prey

There are very few animals out on the sand. Gerbils and other small **rodents** venture across the surface to find seeds. But it is impossible to dig burrows in the sand, so these animals have to find firmer ground to make their burrows. Geckos and skinks hunt on the surface for scorpions and insects.

### Explorer's notes

**Adaptations** of small desert mammals:
- shelter by day in burrows
- **nocturnal**
- obtain water from their food.

The yellow scorpion raises its sting to warn off predators.

## Movement
The horned viper moves across the sand in a side-winding movement, like the sidewinder rattlesnake of North American deserts.

## Buried predator

You watch a skink hurry over the hot surface. Suddenly, there is a flurry of sand and the skink is caught in the jaws of a horned viper. This **venomous** snake lies buried to trap its **prey**. It quickly swallows its catch and buries itself. The snake's wedge-shaped head and flat body help it to dive below the surface, where the sand is cool. This snake feels the vibrations in the sand made when the prey animal crosses the surface.

The horned viper can dig quickly into the sand.

# The amazing camel

Your desert exploration would have been impossible without the **adaptations** of the animal you have been riding. For a start, it has not had a drink for three days. It can go ten times as long without water as a person can. Back at the pool it would have filled its stomach with up to 150 litres of water.

## Bactrian camel

The Bactrian camel, or two-humped camel, lives in the cold Gobi Desert of Mongolia. Unlike the one-humped Arabian camel, the Bactrian camel has very thick hair all over its body.

**Camels originally came from the desert region of Arabia, east of Africa. They have been used in the Sahara for centuries by the Tuareg people.**

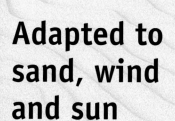

## Adapted to sand, wind and sun

The camel's feet have two toes with skin webbing between. This webbing keeps the camel from sinking into sand. When the wind blows, the camel can shut its nostrils tightly to keep out the sand. The camel's eyelids are like sunshades, protecting the eyes from the blinding light.

This camel's nostrils are shut tight against windblown sand.

### Explorer's notes

Camel adaptations:
- tough mouth for eating thorny plants
- woolly back, which provides protection from the sun
- webbed feet for walking on sand.

# Water in the desert

Your camel ride is over, and now a helicopter takes you to an island of green in the sea of desert sand and gravel. It is an **oasis**, no bigger than a soccer field. Water from deep underground has found its way to the surface where it bubbles out as fresh spring water. There are plants and animals here that would not survive in the desert. Here you find date palms and fruit trees grown by desert people.

**Bou Saada Oued oasis in Algeria has been used by people for centuries.**

# Chotts

**Chotts** are wetlands in the desert formed when rainwater or underground water collects in **depressions**. The water in the chotts is salty because there is salt in the ground in these parts of the Sahara. Many chotts are permanent; others dry out completely. A large number of plants that can live in salty places grow in chotts.

Lake Mavo is a large salt lake in the sand dunes of the Sahara.

## Explorer's notes

Chott animals:
- lesser flamingoes
- white-headed ducks
- four-toed jerboas
- slender-billed curlews.

Chott plants:
- rushweed
- bulrushes
- **algae**
- saltbushes.

27

# Changing desert

The Sahara will not stay the same forever. The dinosaur fossils and the paintings in the desert mountains show that change in the climate turned a lush forest into the desert of today. The climate is still changing – so what will the Sahara be like in the future?

If rainfall increases, more plants will grow and with more plants there will be more animals, and maybe more people. If rainfall decreases and the desert becomes even drier, many animals and plants may not be able to survive.

## Protecting habitats

The desert mountains, **chotts** and **oases** are very important habitats for many animals that would not survive out on the desert dunes and plains. This is why protection of these areas of the Sahara is so important.

# Extinction and survival

Just as hippopotamuses and giraffes died out as the desert formed, the jerboas and fennec foxes may not survive if their desert **habitat** disappears. But such changes are slow, taking place over centuries. Other changes are not so slow. Some animals, such as the scimitar-horned oryx, have almost become **extinct** in just a few decades due to people hunting them.

Explorer's notes

**Endangered** animals of the Sahara:
- scimitar-horned oryx
- slender-horned gazelles
- dama gazelles
- addax
- cheetahs.

**Zoos are breeding endangered Saharan animals, such as the scimitar-horned oryx, to keep them from becoming extinct.**

# Find out for yourself

You may have the opportunity to visit a desert. Observe the different kinds of **habitats** you see. Observe the animals and plants you see in these places. Observe the habitats at different times of the year to find out what changes occur.

## Using the Internet

Explore the Internet to find out more about desert habitats. Websites can change, so if the links below no longer work, don't worry. Use a kid-friendly search engine, such as www.yahooligans.com or www.internet4kids.com, and type in keywords such as 'desert animals', or even the name of a particular desert or animal.

## Websites

http://www.stemnet.nf.ca/CITE/deserts.htm
Find out all about deserts of the world, including desert climate, wildlife and formation.

http://www.projectexploration.org/jobaria.htm
Read interesting information about the jobaria dinosaur.

**Disclaimer**
All the Internet addresses (URLs) given in this book were valid at the time of going to press. However, due to the dynamic nature of the Internet, some addresses may have changed or ceased to exist since publication. While the author and publisher regret any inconvenience this may cause readers, no responsibility for any such changes can be accepted by either the author or the publisher.

# Glossary

**adaptation**  feature of an animal or plant that helps it to survive

**alga**  (plural: algae) plant without roots or sap

**barren**  not able to produce plant growth

**chott**  desert wetland

**dehydrate**  lose water or moisture

**depression**  wide, shallow hole in soil or rock

**evaporate**  turn from liquid to gas when heated

**extinct**  when a type of living thing is no longer living

**fertile**  producing much plant growth

**habitat**  place where animals and plants live

**mammal**  animal that drinks its mother's milk when it is young

**migrate**  move from one place to another

**nocturnal**  active at night

**oasis**  fertile place with water in a desert

**predator**  animal that kills and eats other animals

**prey**  animal that is killed and eaten by other animals

**rodent**  mammal with gnawing teeth. Rats, mice and beavers are rodents.

**species**  group of living things that reproduce with each other

**taproot**  main root of a plant

**venomous**  poisonous

# Index